# Trust Your Gut

## An Autobiography of Reclaiming Intuition

## By Toni Geving

# Trust Your Gut

# An Autobiography of Reclaiming Intuition

Written by Toni Geving

Edited by Julie Pritschet

Copyright © 2019 Toni Geving

All Rights Reserved

No part of this publication may be reproduced or transmitted in any form or by any means, mechanical or electronic, including photocopying and recording, or by any information storage and retrieval system, without permission in writing from the author or publisher.

ISBN: 978-0-9983961-3-2

## Dedications

*I would like to dedicate this book to my mother, Louise. This woman lived for her children, doing everything she could to keep her family safe and whole. I was so blessed to be able to take care of her for the last 5 years of her life as she lived with Alzheimer's. How wonderful it was to have you as my Mom.*

# Acknowledgements

With much love, gratitude and respect, I need to acknowledge the people who have been with me along this last 10 years of life. I must say that I can only attribute my being here to share my story to loving support, whether they thought I was crazy or not!

I could not have published my first book without my siblings. They gave me weekends away from caring for my mom, which allowed me to go to coffee shops and the homes of friends to write. I will appreciate my brother, Craig, for feeding my cat while I was away. I know he is not a lover of the feline, but he understood his importance. This was never more apparent than when I came home from a long weekend and was asked, "Toni, where is your cat? I've been helping Mom look for him all weekend." Apparently, I forgot to tell him that Nova had crossed the "rainbow bridge" two days before. He was respectfully empathetic.

In addition, I must acknowledge my friend and his son. I appreciated you spending your weekends with me and mom for a year. I was so sad that my mother's disease made it difficult for you both. I love you both and missed you when it was time for you to go. I hope that you know that I appreciated the time you spent with us and will always remember the laughter and wish only the best for you.

For my readers, many of them clients and friends, I appreciate you asking me for the next book. I understand this is different than the first one, but I hope you find it as informative. I promise I will continue to write from the heart. Thank you for your support and reviews.

Again, I thank my whole tribe for everything you do. I must say it extended to my art community of friends. Deb and Russell, I hope to work with you both on your stories and help you get them to a point where you will share them. Your friendship was very needed when my family scattered. When I came home, I had people to have dinner with, talk to and shoot ideas around. Although there are always going to be "poop throwing monkeys" please do not let them into your zoo! We all know the truth!

## Introduction

When I wrote my first book "One Without the Other an Autobiography of Grief and Intuition", I had no idea how it would impact the dynamics of relationships with my friends, family and the outside world. I write my story with the intention that someone will learn something about their own story through mine. In addition, I hope that an individual reader will learn something about themselves that will make them evolve into something better. With that, I write from my heart and my own point of view. I do not believe that everyone has the same views as I. As with any accounting of events, what I know to be true may not be the same as others in the fray.

My husband's sister took offense to my first book and projected issues onto me that were not mine to carry. Therefore, his family does not communicate with me anymore, though I have reached out more than once to them. Unfortunately, I cannot resolve their issues for them. I cannot respond to them with the positive intentions I have for them. So, as you read through my words, please know that I do not intend for you to take offense. I intend for you to be honest about how you feel and rather than blame anyone else for those feelings, ask yourself why you feel the way you do. Is it possible that you feel this way because you know there is truth there? Are you missing something in your understanding? I am not asking for you to agree. Just respect that my story is different than yours.

We all have our own story. Mine involves sensitivity to sound and light. I have issues with distractions of the spiritual kind. Let me tell you, we all have a spirit. There is much debate if spirit and soul are the same. From what I have witnessed, they are the same. I do not believe the spirit dies. The physical body goes and the spirit survives. However, that spirit takes on many forms without a body and can be lost or stuck here. Our human experience makes that transition so much worse than it needs to be. If only we could retain the knowledge that our spirit brings into human form, we would not be "tied" to land or space. This book explains how I started exploring this. This book has many conversations with spirit.

I sway in and out of memories from my childhood. I was taught to repress my gifts. I cannot blame my mom. I believe she said what she did to protect her overly-sensitive child. Though, I believe everyone can do what I do. I think that we choose not to speak to spirit and call it "unholy". I will argue that if you speak to God, Allah, Buhda, or any other higher power, you are speaking to

Spirit. For those of you who pull out your Bible to bear testimony against mystics, remember that you are condemning yourself. I have no problem praying. I have no problem having conversation with God. So, why should I have a problem speaking to Spirit, which is all part of God? It is all from the same source.

I still talk to Spirit every day. I see angels, passed loved ones, pets, and horrifyingly evil things, for which I call in protection, and more. We all have the choice between working for a higher outcome of love, or the lower outcome of hate. We all have free will. Quit blaming your choice on the Devil Tempting you! We are all tempted! You have the ability to choose. The words you say, the actions you take, the life you live are all choices like the clothes you wear. Are you choosing to nourish your highest self? Are you choosing to uplift your neighbor? Or, are you tearing them down with your projection of your choice?

I hope you enjoy this next part of my story. It was hard won.

Toni Geving
August 29, 2019
Minnesota

# Chapter 1

When a loved one dies, the individuals left behind may struggle for many months to figure out how to continue through their life without that person that was so much a part of it. The phases of the grieving process co-mingle and weave through each other like a ball of tangled string. Even though you may find the end of the string, pulling that end only creates knots and tension in the middle that will take you hours, days, weeks, or even months or years to disentangle and work out. At least, this was the best way I could describe my own grieving process when my husband died in 2009. It's not just sadness and heartache that plagued me, but anger, guilt, regret and envy wound their way through the mess of emotions. With the added bonus of a traumatic brain injury and the reintroduction of my intuitive gifts, I learned to question everything... repeatedly.

Then, just as I thought I had a handle on the grieving, my best friend died. All of a sudden, the stages of grief are even more mixed up and tangled. My anger towards Cally for not going to the doctor and saying, "I think it's my liver," became anger towards John. Or, I would become angry with Cally because she was where John was and was able do stuff with him, while I stayed home. There were days when my depression at losing my two best friends was so deep that I wanted to go to bed and never get up. While, other days, I knew I had to get out of the house because, if I didn't, John would sit there and heckle me the whole time. I did not want anyone else to know how much I was hurting. Nor, did I want to be supportive to anyone else and their pain. Looking back, I know that I wanted to save others from my lashing out. John's family and Cally's family were grieving too. I was not in a place to be supportive, even though I knew that I could be. In the midst of all of this, I was also waning in and out of my own pity party. I certainly didn't need anyone else to extend their pity to me.

Although I had no anger towards any of John's family, many of the things said and done before and after John's death hurt me. Even though John and I came together with very different backgrounds, we were very well-suited for each other. Each of our strengths and weaknesses complimented the other. But, New Richmond was a small town full of people who knew the Gevings, and inevitably, something would come back to me from someone who talked to someone else. It was no secret that I was not liked by a couple of John's siblings. Nothing became more evident than that fact when John died. I had been talking to Jeff and forgave him for his words the night of John's death. I truly believe he understood how much I loved his brother, whether he liked me or not. And, I cared enough about his family to try and hide my hurt. For the most part, I don't even think any of them remember half the crap that they spew out of their mouths. John understood that and used to tell me, "Why do you care what they say or think about us? It isn't about us at all. That is about them and how they feel about themselves."

"Why do you not care? They tear you and I down like we are beneath them!" I asked.

"Let it go, Toni!" he said. "It doesn't matter. I love you. You love me. That is what matters."

He was right. John had more wisdom than anyone gave him credit for and he could call anyone on their crap in an instant. More often than not, he would just let them talk their talk and self-destruct. He would give minimal argument and just go about doing what he was going to do. He knew that everyone had their own version of the truth.

It was all this turmoil that was causing me most of my anxiety then. I didn't want to get into it with anyone about the things that were said to me, about me, or to John. I didn't want to cause any pain to them. I knew they were grieving as much as I was and I just didn't want to say something that would cause more of the same. I did not want my emotional cluster bomb to explode into a blame game. They were not responsible for John's death. They were not responsible for how I felt, any more than I was responsible for how they felt. So, I did not call them to talk about John. I did not share my grieving with them.

In August of 2010, I was expecting a very important delivery that I had been anticipating for almost 9 months. Finally, I received the call from Lifegem™; the company in Chicago where I had sent 8 ounces of my husband's cremated remains in January. My diamonds were ready to be shipped to me. Due to the value of this purchase, I needed to be home to sign for the package. I was given a delivery timeframe between 9:00 AM and 3:00 PM. Naturally, I took the whole day off from my full-time job to wait for Federal Express to ring my doorbell.

Anyone who knows me well understands that I am not the most patient person in the world. I realized that there was some sort of lesson in patience that I was missing, as I seemed to constantly be in some sort of holding pattern, waiting for something, or someone. So, sitting in my two-bedroom apartment all day was difficult for me. I was not alone. I had already learned that we are never really alone. The shroud of time is thin enough for anyone to see through. The past year had proved that I excelled at looking through the shroud at what was and what will be. On that day in August, I chatted with Spirit while I intermittently cleaned, cried, and prayed.

During one of the moments when I was crying, I realized that the tears running down my face were entirely about grieving the loss of my husband and not related to the anxiety I felt about spending the money on the diamonds. I had already had my year of firsts without John. But, the two anniversaries that put me into an emotional state that was close to crippling were my wedding anniversary and the anniversary of his death. My wedding anniversary was August 31$^{st}$, and John was not there. I only had ten years with him and seven of them were after we wed. I became a widow at 41 years of age.

One of the things that I had done for the past year was to look at the parallels between my experience and that of others. More specifically, I made a comparison of my experience with the death of my spouse and my mom's experience with the death of my father. When my father died, both he and my mother were 44 years of age. My husband, John, was 43 years old. Both my father and my husband died unexpectedly. My father died in his sleep of a presumed heart attack. My husband died in a car accident after losing consciousness at the wheel. Mom had 5 children living at home that were as young as 5 and as old as 20. My daughter, Brooke, was 18 and living with us at the time of her father's death. Mom and Dad had just celebrated their twenty-fifth wedding anniversary and I had only celebrated 7 years of marriage. By this time, I believed that there were no coincidences and that I was supposed to learn something from these parallels. I was supposed to learn something from my mother.

One of the most deep-seated memories I had from my father's death was the wake. I remember being at a funeral home with people coming and going. My father was in a room in a casket that was open. It was late in the evening when my mom came and got me and my little sister, Angie, bringing us up to the casket. My father looked like he was sleeping, but he wasn't snoring. He was clothed in a dark suit jacket. Mom knelt by the casket with two curly-haired girls flanking her sides. When she stood, she said, "It's time to kiss your father good-bye. You won't be seeing him for a long time."

She held each of us up so we could bend and kiss our father's cheek. I remember the feel of his cold skin, the smell from the embalming and the protest I made when she said I had to kiss him. "But, he's not in there Mommy, he's standing over there," I whispered, pointing across the room. That only seemed to make her mad because she gave me "the look" that all mothers give you when you are in trouble.

"Toni Marie, give your father a kiss good-bye," she whispered in a scolding tone.

When I asked her about this memory later, she did not remember making me kiss him. She did not remember scolding me in a whisper. Yet, she did remember me stating he was standing on the other side of the room. Even with my head injury, I remembered it for years afterward and as a result, I made John promise to not let anyone see my dead body less than a month before he died. Now, I understand that my mom was still in shock. She was still trying to figure out what she was going to do without her life partner. How was she going to make it work with 4 children under 18 at home on a part-time salary?

After John died, I asked her what I said when I called her to tell her. She explained that I told her that John was in an accident. When she asked me if he was okay, I responded, "No. He's dead." She told me that I was not crying and that my voice had no emotion when I told her. It was so unlike me to not be emotional. Before my head injury, I was very sensitive to everything. In 2009,

I did not have the emotional part of my brain functioning. In truth, I did not have any part of my brain functioning normally. Regardless of the brain injury, I had no recollection of how I told her of his death.

As I sat on my couch that August day, I wondered what I was learning from these two important male figures dying and what I was supposed to learn from my mother. Why did I draw the short straw? I realize that I had a lot of thoughts in that timeframe that started out with "why me". It felt like God was purposely forcing me to do this on my own. Granted, I had support in my family, but it wasn't the same as having someone to make decisions with you. Yet, there were only a few of those people with whom I trusted enough to share my gifts. My school friends were fine with me telling them I saw dead people, angels, and the like. My immediate family was not so receptive. Or, my fear of losing them because of a conflict in our beliefs kept me quiet. I can say now that it was more likely the later of these two statements that represented the truth.

By the time FedEx showed up at my door, I was over my pity party and excited to see my diamonds. I'd been talking to spirit most of the day, but John did not show up until FedEx did. I could feel his energy as I grabbed the box cutter to open the box, wondering what kind of super glue they used on their adhesive these days.

My father was there, too. "Slow down and steady your hands or you are going to cut yourself!" he warned.

I realized he was right when I noticed my hands were shaking. After a couple deep breaths, I was calmer and able to cut through the box lid. Then, I found the tear off tab on the opposite side of the box. "Dammit!" I said aloud, as I noticed it.

"You would have torn it off anyway," John teased.

When I finally got the box opened, I took out a folder of paperwork, and two white gift boxes. They looked like jewelry boxes and had the LifeGem™ logo on them. I opened one of the lids on the box and found another box with a clear lid inside. Beneath the lid, a round cut peridot-green colored stone winked at me. My breath caught as I felt the warmth of my husband's embrace at that very moment. "Oh my God," I whispered, "it is beautiful!"

"I am partial to the green one, but you are going to like the yellow one better," John said.

I was not done looking at the green one and pulled the acrylic box out of the white cardboard one. The box itself was pretty cool, although, it looked like a little coffin with a woodgrain finish. Afraid of losing the diamond that I had worked so hard to purchase, I kept the stone in the box and took off my engagement ring. In one hand I held the box with the clear lid and diamond and my engagement ring in the other, I tried comparing the size of the stones. They were both approximately a third of a karat. My intention was to have them set together with my wedding bands. They would work.

When I was done examining the green stone, I unlidded the yellow one. John was right. I did like that one better. It was a beautiful canary yellow and princess cut. It was absolutely gorgeous! This was the one I intended to have put into a pendant that I could wear close to my heart. I loved them both.

"Toni," John said, "you cannot give one of these to Brooke for a long time."

"I know."

"I mean it. The promise Theresa and I made to her about Theresa's engagement ring is not your concern. We made the promise, not you."

"I know. But you know how I am about promises!"

"Yes. Don't make them and break them. I know who you are."

As I looked at the stones, feeling John's arm around me, I started to cry again. I was feeling overwhelmed by it all. I knew that money was tight for me and I had just spent quite a bit of money on these diamonds. I wasn't regretting the decision. Just wanted to make sure I worked hard enough to get them in settings that I could wear. I would have to wait awhile before I could do that.

Because of the alcohol in John's toxicology report on his autopsy, I did not receive any insurance payout for the accidental death clause of his life insurance policy. Most of the time, it is the accidental death side of life insurance that carries the most money. So, buying these diamonds came almost entirely out of my pocket. I had used the majority of the financial payout on the other half of John's small life policy to pay off the funeral expenses, make down payments on three different cars, and a couple other things. It was enough to help supplement the loss of John's salary for a year. But, his life was worth more than any amount of money. I would have given everything I had to have him here.

"I had to go, Toni," he reminded me. "It was just time for me to go."

"No, it was more than that," I whispered to him, "and I know it."

"I think you should set that yellow one in a round setting," John told me. "I have always been the square peg to your round hole."

"Or, I was the square one."

In October, I actually had the square cut diamond mounted into a round bezel in a heart pendant. My mistake was not buying a chain for the pendant. The only one I had at home was sterling silver and it turned my neck green when I wore it. I had the green diamond set with our wedding bands and my engagement ring in a ring, which I could wear when I was not massaging. I wore it quite often to my full-time job. It was heavy and shaped like an infinity symbol because my love for him would always be present, no matter what happened.

Every few months, John would remind me of the promise I made to him about getting married again. At the same time, I would remind him that the option to meet someone, fall in love and get married was not entirely my decision. Honestly, I was not sure that I wanted to be as vulnerable with someone else. I didn't want to put my heart out there and have to grieve the loss of someone else. Plus, it was entirely too soon for me to even consider making myself available for dating. I had no desire to date anyone. I was still in love with my husband, who was dead, but very much present in my life.

There was also the loss of Cally, my best friend. She was still hanging around on occasion. Often times, she would come in with John and I would smell her flowery sweetness and his Old Spice mixed together. I imagine they were having some party in the afterlife. But, I think they both came together because they knew I was hurting and alone that year. I didn't reach out to people, though Bill and I would hang out, have dinner, or just watch television. As much as I wanted to have a social life, I didn't want it to be in New Richmond.

I liked my independence and was becoming more accustomed to living alone with my cat, but knew there was something missing. I got up, went to work, came home, went to work, came home, ate, watched television and played on Facebook, going to bed later. Some days, I would paint or draw. But I had not done anything serious enough that I wanted to frame it. I was stuck in a pattern of forced existence, because I still was trying to figure out why I was the one living and talking to dead people.

Yes, that was the truth. I talked to dead people. I also talked to angels and demons on occasion, Jesus and other spirit beings. In late 2010, I was beginning to realize, I was talking to my cat and he was answering me, too. For some reason, he had a French accent. I have no clue how that works. Nova Scotia was named after a Canadian province, but I don't think he was from there and have no clue if any part of that area is French speaking. My curiosity about his accent made me look up Nova Scotia, only to find that the French settlers were expelled by the British in the late eighteen hundreds. However, there was a dialect of French that was compared to the Louisiana Cajun French. So, maybe he was French after all?

# Chapter 2

On New Year's Day 2011, I received a call from my sister-in-law, Karla, to come to a new bar in downtown New Richmond, WI and have a drink with her and Jeff. Although Jeff and I had our differences, we had come to an understanding and mutual appreciation for each other's friendship. He even apologized for lashing out at me when he was grieving. I completely forgave him, as I understood what it was to feel emotions so intensely and not be able to express them. Plus, it was a misunderstanding of my intention that caused the issue to begin with, as my brain gave me concern with sound. For me, my anger became sadness, while Jeff was exactly opposite. So, when the call came to meet them, I decided I would go to the new place.

Brady's Brewhouse was a place John would have loved. It had open concept dining and a bar, with 40 beers on tap, a brewery in the back and some really good food. There were antique trinkets and a retro-cool pulley system operating the ceiling fans. As I plopped myself down on a bar stool, I took in the atmosphere and knew I liked it. It was about 11:30 in the morning on a Sunday and because it was a holiday, I had the next day off at work, as did Jeff and Karla. This was great because we would be there until the next day. We did not leave until after midnight. We laughed, drank, ate, watched football and did more of the laughing, drinking and eating. In fact, I left about 9, only to come back with Bill.

This day with Jeff and Karla was very important in a couple ways. The first was that we built a friendship that day. Karla and I had already established our sisterhood. Yet, it took the death of John to make Jeff and I realize that we both loved him and would keep his memory alive truthfully. We all grieve in our own ways and our own time. Jeff was doing his grieving like I was. I respected that his grief was different than mine.

The second thing that came from that day was a decision to stay in New Richmond for a bit longer. New Richmond was John's town. He grew up there. He knew everyone, or they knew someone in his family. His family was there. Plus, the memories I made with John were in this town and I was still coming to terms with them.

For some reason, I felt that I was responsible for keeping John's memory alive for his friends, family and myself. In fact, I had many conversations with him about that very thing. He would sit there and listen. Then, he would say, "You are not responsible for making everyone remember me. They will remember what they will. Though, you remember a lot more now than you will admit."

"That is true," I said. "However, I never know if what I am remembering is real. There is so much that feels like I had a dream about it."

"Trust your gut, Toni!"

"I am trying to do that, but it still kind of freaks me out that I see and hear things that nobody else hears or sees."

Again, John nodded his head. He understood my fears. He was part of the reason I started to reclaim my gifts. When my head injury took my short-term memory, I started to remember things from my childhood and heard the voices of people long gone. Angels and spirit beings were everywhere and I could hear them and see them. It wasn't until he died and came to see me that first time that I understood exactly what was happening. It had been two years since I had fallen on New Year's Day and bashed my head. So, as I sat there on the barstool, I felt that it was the anniversary of my decision to stay. I made a decision to stay in this life in 2009. On January 1st, 2011, I made a decision to stay in that town and learn some more from the Spirits that were constantly there.

"Yeah, I like this place," John said in my ear, towards the end of the night.

"I knew you would," I thought.

"Now that Jeff knows you like Long Island's, you need to let him take you out more often. You are never going to meet your husband sitting at home."

"What are you talking about?"

"Toni," he said, with a warning tone, "you made a promise to me. Remember?"

"Oh for the love of God, John," I thought, exasperated. "Do you really expect me to be out trolling for men because I made you a promise before you died? Doesn't death wipe that slate clean?"

I hear the laughter in his voice as he said, "No. You know that a promise is a promise."

Because I wasn't about to start talking out loud to him in a crowded bar, I decided to remind him of his promise to me. "You are supposed to send him to me, remember? It takes more than me looking."

"Okay, I get that. I'm glad you are out though."

"I am too," I admitted.

"He's coming. You still have things to learn, but you will know when you are ready. Trust that gut of yours."

"Tonay!" Jeff called from two seats away. "Do you need another Long Island?"

For as long as I could remember, I had acquired nicknames wherever I was. Some of the earlier ones were from my maiden name. It amused me that Jeff pronounced my name "toe-nay" because some of the most hilarious nicknames came from the mispronunciation of my names. I had a friend in Texas that called me Malone. In fact, she picked me up at the Houston airport one time and had me paged. "Passenger Toni Malone, please pick up a white courtesy phone."

Then, when I worked in loss prevention in the Mall of America, I started getting court documents from the Hennepin County Court System addressed to "Mystic Decknadel." Apparently, someone called and asked who the Loss Prevention Manager was and the caller was told "Miss Toni Decknadel". The miss and Toni became Mystic. My regional manager called me Mystic for months after that one.

My husband rarely called me Toni. In fact, his nickname for me was "Dear" or "Hey". He used my name more often posthumously than he did while he was alive.

For some reason, I believe that was because I called him "Johnny" like his family did and he did not like that. In fact, he told me he didn't want me to call him Johnny. We had many discussions about that, but he never told me why. In retrospect, I admitted that I called him that more often around his friends and family because they called him that. His spirit denied it, but I was pretty sure that was his way of annoying me.

When Jeff started calling me "Toe-nay", I felt it was his way of showing me some form of acceptance. That was his greeting most of the time when I saw him. He just called me from across the room with the elongated mispronunciation of my name. However, I wondered if we would continue to be friends as we developed our new normal without John.

Anyone who has ever married understands that when they get married, they do not just marry a person. They really do marry the family. For better or worse, they become part of the family and all of their stories. Some of those relationships work well, while others do not. In addition, every family has their own dysfunction and their own code, or set of rules by which they live. Some of those familial differences have brought couples together. John and I had many discussions about this because we both felt like outsiders in our respective families. We both loved our families, but never felt like we fit in them. So, while I wanted to still be a part of this family, I did not know how to do that and fulfill my promise to John.

With that in mind, I began the year with the intention to separate myself from the family functions. I stopped going to the family get-togethers for major holidays. Although I understood that John's family wanted my happiness and would be happy for me if I found someone to share them with, I did not want to split my holiday time between families and I did not want to expect any new partner to accommodate my late husband's family. It was hard enough going to all the family Christmases when John was alive! It seemed we were never creating our own traditions, but always alternating the traditions of everyone else. John had always wanted to be around people, while I liked having my alone time. But, here I was going out with Jeff and Karla. From this family where I was an outsider, I gained friends.

I had another Long Island with Jeff and ended up going home after midnight. As I settled into my bed, my cat came and snuggled with me. He had been waiting for me- his only human servant. As I closed my eyes and let go of another piece of John, I cried into the fur of my cat and ignored the voices that continued to talk to me.

The Monday holiday was quiet at the apartment. I stayed in bed until 11:00, put a load of laundry into the washer and sat down with my journal, a cup of coffee and a pen. It was time to talk to the angels and set some intentions for my year. I needed to change something. I needed to move over to a more productive way of thinking. I needed to be open to the things that my heart needed.

"You need to get married again," John told me as I started my intentions.

"That is not on my list for this year," I told him out loud. When I was alone, I started to speak to Spirit out loud. Speaking it out loud made the experience more real and honest for me. I was beginning to remember the gifts that I had repressed for so many years. I was beginning to remember the Spirits I had relationships with that nobody else knew about. I was beginning to remember why I repressed my gifts in the first place. I believed then, if people heard me talking to Spirit in public, they would automatically assume that I was schizophrenic, or mentally deranged. Hell, sometimes, I thought I *was* having some type of psychotic episode.

"You know that you need to start going out more. You don't get out enough."

"John," I said in exasperation, "Stop pushing me! You know I am not ready yet. Plus, I told you that I cannot make that happen by myself."

"I told you I would help you."

"Then, quit heckling me and help me! I will go out more this year," I explained, "but I am not going to be picking up men in bars."

"Create an online profile again."

"Please stop."

The whole conversation was verbal and I was beginning to feel argumentative. I didn't want to really talk to him and I told him that mentally. It was then that I realized that Archangel Michael was there. He raised his arm and silenced John's replay with a shake of his head. As I had come to associate John with the Sword of Michael, I associated this gesture as a "resting of the sword." He pulled John back from his attack, as the sword was what was cutting away the energy that was not serving my highest good. It should not have been inflicting pain on me.

"Allow her to set her intentions and get out of her way," he said. "She is right. If you really want to help her, you may only present the opportunities for her."

When I started writing this chapter, I looked for the journal that had my 2011 intentions. In doing so, I realized that it was in the box of books that incurred water damage in one of my moves. I had stored the box in a storage facility and had 15 inches of melted snow and ice come down through a ceiling onto it and my couch. Everything in the box was a loss and thrown away. So, I do not recall all of my intentions for that year. However, there were three that I do remember. The first was that I intended to find my peace with being alone and not being lonely. Second, I intended to incorporate my gifts into my business. And, third, I intended to make room for someone to share my life.

It was not until April that I started to consider how I would incorporate my ability to speak with Spirits and angels into my business. The confidence I had in my ability to do this for others was not as big as I felt it should be. Yet, my guides and angels were pushing me to help others by sharing messages with them. In addition, they told me that I could start drawing their likeness for others. "I cannot draw," I argued.

"Yes, you can. You are a gifted artist."

"Stick figures can be drawn by anyone!"

"You are being too hard on yourself," said Tammy, one of my angel cheerleaders. "You will create imagery that speaks to others and we will give you the information they need for their healing."

"Trust is difficult for me," I admitted. "My gifts have brought me a lot of grief in this lifetime."

"In others too," Tammy confirmed. "Just start painting."

In 2010, I had created a couple watercolor images to help me heal. Art was always healing for me. Watercolor had enough accidental brilliance that I found it beautiful. But, I knew that I could not just paint guides. It took too much time. I would start a painting and not finish it for months. I would throw some paint on the paper and come back to it. My studio was in my living room and sometimes, a painting would get dusty because I left it for so long. Some paintings would go unfinished for years. I told all of this to Tammy.

"You need to try soft pastel," she suggested.

"The chalk stuff?"

"Yes. It blends well and will get your hands dirty."

"I will look into it," I agreed.

That year, I painted a portrait of my lovely friend, Cally. I ended up giving it to her mom, as it felt right. I started to paint John too. However, I never finished his painting. I could not get his mouth right. Tammy told me it was because I wanted him to stop talking to me. "You are tired of him pushing you and unconsciously, you don't want to give him a mouth."

I had to laugh because I was sure she was correct. "Unfortunately, he doesn't need one to talk to me."

"True," she agreed, "But, he can be obnoxious."

"For you too?" I laughed.

"He's still learning and has good intentions."

"He certainly learned how to talk!"

I heard John laughing after I said that. I used to tell him and others that "John wouldn't say shit if he had a mouth full of it." Now, I couldn't get him to shut up. Even though he was there laughing, he did not say anything.

"I think you should offer readings," another guide spoke up. "Tell people about the Spirits that are with them and give them direct messages. If you want, you can buy some of those oracle cards and use them to give messages."

"I don't know," I wavered. "How do I market that? I mean, my family already thinks I am a freak."

"They do not!" he protested.

"They don't believe in this stuff."

"You would be surprised. They may not believe that you possess the gift, because you have hidden it for so long. However, I am sure they know you are telling the truth, as each of them have their own abilities. They may choose not to work with them, as you have. You have accepted this is part of your life contract."

"Does that really exist?" I asked. I had read and heard from other intuitives about life contracts. What I had heard and read was that we decide our lessons before we come into human form. I had a difficult time accepting that I would choose to have so much loss in my lifetime. I could not believe that I would choose to learn lessons this way. Yet, the life contract also includes your commitment to purpose, as everyone has a life purpose.

"Well, yes," Archangel Haniel affirmed.

"So, do past lives exist?" I asked. "Did we evolve from monkeys? Is God a monkey?" I was only half kidding. I really wanted to talk to the points of evolution and past lives. Yet, Haniel was not going to entertain me. He was putting me back on topic.

"Yes, there is a life contract. But, your contract changes in every lifetime, though your lesson may not change, it is presented differently." He was gentle, but firm when he responded to this. Then, with a smile, he said, "God is not a monkey."

# Chapter 3

By the end of June, I was ready to start opening up to the idea of having a new partner in my life. I did not feel like I was ever going to get married, but I wanted companionship with someone of the male gender that was not connected with John. I loved the friendships I had with John's high school buddies, but I needed someone who was not part of my story of grief. Having grieved with his family and friends, I was not sure how to get beyond grieving if I did not have something that was not a part of it.

One of my many healing friends suggested that I start doing some Feng shui in my apartment to make room for a new love. The suggestions I received ranged from making room in my closet for someone else, adding a nightstand to the other side of the bed, and rearranging my room.  The first thing I decided was that I did not want anyone new sleeping in John's spot.  I needed to get used to sleeping on the opposite side of the bed.

When John and I got married, we traded beds with my Mom.  I had a queen- sized bed and my mom had a king, which was in need of a new mattress.  I agreed to give my mom my queen four-post bed if I could have her king frame and box spring.  John was sleeping on a twin bed while we were going out.  So, when we got married and shared a bed, he had to get used to having more space.  Due to his small bed, he had developed the ability to launch himself up in the air, flip over to a different position and flop back down, launching me into the air like a catapult.  For a year after we were married, this was his way of turning over in bed, earning him the nickname of "Flipper."  I believed this was how dolphins would flip in the air.

In addition, John was not someone who liked to cuddle.  In fact, he could not stand having anything touch him while he slept.  So, we had an imaginary line down the middle of the bed while we slept.  It was kind of like children in the backseat of a car on a road trip.  Once we kissed each other goodnight and were going to sleep, we didn't touch unless it was accidentally.  As I tend to fall off to sleep immediately and not move for the night, Flipper would be the only one encroaching onto my side of the bed. Though, we had many playful arguments about this.

As most couples who share a bed do, each individual has a preference on which side of a double bed they like to sleep. When we were married, I gave up the side I normally slept on while single to accommodate John's preference. After he died, it took me two and a half years to feel comfortable sleeping on that imaginary line. It reminded me of the movie *When Harry Met Sally*, when Harry's character asked Sally if she still slept on the same side of the bed. When she said she used to but she then was "pretty much using the whole bed," Harry responded, "God, that's great. I feel weird when just my leg crosses over." That was exactly how I felt about sleeping on the line- weird.

The night that I decided to just switch sides, John showed up to heckle me. "What are you doing?"

"Going to bed," I said plainly.

"Aren't you on the wrong side?" he asked, with humor in his voice.

"I don't think so."

"Um, that is my side of the bed."

"What? That is ridiculous!"

"Why is it ridiculous?" he asked.

"Because you are dead," I reasoned, "a state of permanent rest. You do not need to sleep."

"That is totally beside the point." I could hear the humor in his voice.

"No," I argued, "that is completely the point!"

"I do not follow your logic."

"You are the one who said I should get married again, right?"

"Well, yes."

"Well, John, this is a large bed, but there is not enough room for you, me and a new spouse."

"Well, the new spouse is not here yet."

"Neither are you, in case you have forgotten."

I could hear the amusement in his voice when he said, "Obviously, I am here. You are talking to me. You can see me. You can hear me…"

"It's not your side of the bed anymore!" I interrupted.

"It is."

"Okay. Would you rather that I sleep on this side? Or, my future spouse?" I could not believe I was arguing with him like we used to do. He wasn't really concerned with me sleeping on his side of the bed. He just wanted to push my buttons and make me explain why I was doing this.

"Well, when you put it that way..." he trailed off. Then, I could hear his laughter, as if he physically was in the room. In fact, Nova, my cat, jumped at the sound. Then, Nova got up from where he had been sprawled on the bed, walked over to John and started rubbing up against him to receive his ghostly petting. I had seen him do this before, but at that moment, it was all so surreal. If anyone else had come into the room, they would think the cat was rubbing up against thin air.

"It's not your side of the bed anymore," I said again, with a new understanding. I was switching to the opposite side of the bed so that whoever was coming in would feel comfortable. I dared to believe that someone new would be sleeping in my bed. I was beginning to realize that I wanted to have someone to share my bed. I wanted someone with whom to share the rest of my life. I wanted someone who would love me as much, or more, than John did. And, at that moment, John was teasing me because that was part of what I missed about him. He was teasing me so that I would remember some of the things that we did not have that I still could have. I could find a man who liked to cuddle. I wanted a man who would cuddle and hold me into the night, when I was fighting demons in the spirit world. I wanted a man who was strong enough to anchor my body and magnetically pull my soul back to him.

"Geez," John smiled while petting the cat, "that took you long enough!

"You suck!" I said- kind of angry that he knew all along what I needed to realize on my own. "How did you know? You made me promise before you died?"

The laughter in his eyes softened to something more compassionate and he said, "I knew you better than you know yourself. You love easily and consistently. I always knew you would be true to me. With all of my failures and challenges, you encouraged me and called me on my shit. You knew when I was lying and loved me anyway. You knew I was not perfect and loved me anyway. And, you rescued me many times, even when I let you down. You need someone who will do the same for you, Toni. You need someone to take care of you in a way that I didn't, or couldn't."

"A soft place to land." It was only a whisper, but I knew that was what he was talking about. My life had become so chaotic with the rebirth of my intuition and the death of my two best friends. I just wanted someone to hold me. I wanted someone who was willing to love me for who I was, understand that I was being called to do the work of a medium and help others see that death was not the final outcome. I needed someone that I did not have to save or take care of, but who would take care of me. My friend, Tara, had told me that was her wish for me. Yet, I could not quite grasp what that meant. I was afraid to wish for that because I didn't want to be disappointed if I only had it for a minute and it was gone.

"Yes," the confirmation came from more than one voice. It wasn't just John agreeing with me, but my father, grandfathers, angels and guides. A chorus of voices breathed that one word into the room.

"He is coming Toni," Archangel Michael told me, "but you still have work to do and there will still be heart ache."

"Shit!" I swore. "When is the heartache going to stop?"

"When you have learned what you need to learn," said Timothy, my guardian angel. "Just keep the faith. You will get through it all."

"But I want to get through it all now!" I did not whine it like I wanted to do, but it was close enough. "Why does the hard stuff have to be so drawn out? Why can't you just give it all to me at once? I mean, learn all the crappy stuff and then, I could live a happy life."

There was laughter at that and John said, "You are the strongest woman I know and even with losing me and Cally, you are hopeful. But, do you really think you would grow at all if you would lose more at the same time?"

"Probably not," I admitted. As if losing my husband and my best friend a year apart were not enough heartache to last me for another 42 years, I knew there was more on the way to me. My daughter, Brooke, seemed to hate me most of the time. Not to mention that I lived in a town where whenever someone said anything negative about me, it came back to me through a client or acquaintance of one of my in-laws. I quit taking stock in the idle gossip that got back to me through the network of friends of friends in New Richmond. Anyone who knew me at all could figure out that the gossip was obviously more about the insecurity of the person saying it than an actual character flaw of mine. Yet, it still hurt to know that people I cared about could be so underhanded and two-faced. They never talked to me directly, which again, has nothing to do with my character.

"Toni," John said, "You know that you cannot win with them." He knew who I was thinking about and what they were saying. "I realize it is difficult to stay quiet when they are lashing out at you. You know, they think they are right and they hunt in a pack."

I sighed before I acknowledged him. "They treated you the same way. You and Jeff were never right. Your dad was an awful person. According to them, I am an awful person, too."

"We know better, "Archangel Raziel said. "Sometimes, people put others down to make themselves feel better. It really isn't about you. Your words or actions make them recognize their feelings."

"It just gets tiring to always be the recipient of their poison. I have not done anything to warrant the treatment I have received," I complained.

"True," the chorus sang.

"When it is their time to face their life review, they will have their own atonement, as will you," another archangel said. "The difference is that you do not respond in the like. You may tell people what was said and what happened, but you are not lashing out at them."

"What's the point?" John asked. "It doesn't matter what anyone thinks about you. All that matters is that you loved me and supported me and my daughter. And, Brooke will come around."

As I looked around, I realized that more angels had appeared in my bedroom. I was trying to get to bed. I really could not stay up all night talking angelspeak and be functional the next morning. It was Saturday and I had clients. So, I crawled into John's side of the bed. He leaned down and kissed my forehead, making it tingle a little. "Dream of rainbows," he told me, as he used to tell Brooke.

"John, get to work. You need to find me a partner," I said sleepily.

"Yeah, John," said Timothy. "It really is your job!" All of a sudden, the heckler was getting heckled by angels. I was grateful.

## Chapter 4

Throughout 2011, I began to form an idea of what it was I wanted. I was still working full-time at the insurance company and there were days when I was ready to pack up and go. We would get 20 temporary employees in, completely trained, and then, the company would let half of them go, only to hire 10 more two weeks later. It was frustrating. I never understood the logic behind it. Why would any company spend $20K to train someone for three months? It could not just be to save on benefits after making them full-time regular employees. It was a game of numbers and a totally crappy way of managing people. Granted, the financial aspects during the recession of 2001-2013 hit many companies hard, but managing people like cattle made me ill. These people had families, too. Most of them were qualified to do the work and did their best. Again, the reality that I was just one number, in a room full of many who would jump at the chance to bury me for my job, was overwhelming.

Aside from realizing that I was ready to leave my current job, I also came to understand that I didn't want to work for any company that treated me like a number. In fact, I was pretty sure that I did not want to work for anyone other than myself. Gone were the days of working for the same company for twenty years because of loyalty. Companies just didn't care about their employees that way. Why should I have any loyalty to any employer who would fire me if I took a couple extra days off when my spouse died? Why would I give that employer my tools and skills when they required me to re-learn my entire job with no support from them? Why would I stay eight years with an employer who would fire me because a client told them to do so? Why would I stay with an employer who put more value on getting a customer off of the phone in 3 minutes than it did on being patient with a customer and explaining everything the first time, so they did not have to call back again?

The first answer that came to me was obviously about having some type of financial stability. No matter how I looked at it, this job that I hated paid the rent. Breaking into that egg, I realized it was just plain fear. I was absolutely terrified that I would end up without money, food, a vehicle to get me to a job and a place to live. I was afraid of being alone and homeless. I was afraid of being a complete failure. It was fear that was stopping me.

"Where is your faith?" I asked my reflection in the mirror the day I realized that I had been living in fear. "What did you do when you were afraid and going into the dark as a child? You turned on the damn light!"

My guardian angel, Timothy, came into the bathroom, where I was chastising my reflection and nodded. "You have never been a coward," he told me. "Even as a child you would stare down a demon until it understood you were not afraid."

"Huh?" I asked surprised.

"Yes," he confirmed, nodding his head. "It was that time your brother was hiding under the bed waiting for you. He scared you when he reached up and grabbed you."

"Yeah, I remember that incident. But, I ran screaming from the room."

"True. But, you came back and went to bed with Angela." He waited until I acknowledged him with a nod of my head and then went on, "after you both had fallen asleep, you heard something in the room and woke. You knew something was there before you woke up because it came through your dream."

"Why don't I remember this?" I asked him.

"I think you blocked it out as a way of coping," Timothy explained. "Or, your father helped you by soothing you."

"What happened?" I asked.

"He was standing above Angie. You sat up and stared him down with a determined strength. You even told him, in Hebrew, that in the name of God, he was unwelcome."

"Hebrew?" I questioned. "I do not know Hebrew."

Timothy laughed a little before he said, "You do not remember what you know."

"But, how could I forget a language?"

"Few people understand Spirit. But, that is not the point I am making here." He shook his head a little and waved a hand to quiet my questions. "The point is," he continued, "you stared that demon down like you would jump it if he did anything to Angela. In fact, you told him that whatever he did to those you loved would be returned to him tenfold."

"I actually used the word 'tenfold'?" I asked.

"Yes, but you were speaking with the knowledge from your dream and your past," Timothy explained, as if it made perfect sense to me. "Plus, you had no idea that we were all there with you, including your father. Duke was very protective of his green-eyed monsters."

"I still am," my father said from the hallway.

I looked into the hallway, outside the bathroom door in my apartment and saw several angels standing out there agreeing with Timothy and my father with nods of their heads. "You know," I said, looking pointedly into the bathroom, "it seems a bit crowded in here."

"Toni Marie," my father said, "Even when you lied, you did it with conviction. But, I was so proud of you for staring that demon down even when you were afraid of it. Even as a 9-year-old, you had so much power. Your brother startled you and you turned blue, but you wake up to a demon over your sister and you were ready to give him a fight."

"You turned on the lights," Timothy said. "You summoned angels with a thought and they were there."

"Hah!" I said in disbelief. "You guys just show up."

"Hardly," John said. "I've seen some of your past work."

I shook my head because I was not sure what they were talking about. "What does this have to do with my fear of quitting my job?"

"You aren't going to quit," John informed me. "Towards the end of the year, you will resign because it is good for you and others to go."

It was March and the second anniversary of his death was approaching. I wondered why he was telling me this. I was about to ask him why he seemed to be supporting my decision to leave when he was so opposed to me working my own business full-time while living, when he said, "I was afraid of letting you do that. You made the income, had the insurance, and supported the budget."

Timothy chimed in again, "As you said, where is your faith? You need to have faith, not only in us, but in yourself."

"Your mother did not raise any cowards," my father said.

Mentally, I questioned if that was an accurate statement. I had repressed my gifts for years because of fear. In high school, I had many relationships with spirit that I could not explain to anyone. I lied about these relationships because my real friends would not have understood connecting with something they could not see. I did not tell my friends that I saw dead people, but told stories about the human experience of the spirit, as if they were still alive and living. I lied to my friends because I was afraid of them finding out what I really was. So much so, that when the pressure of hiding my many spiritual relationships became so overwhelming, I lied about why I had headaches and dark circles under my eyes. "I am dying," I had told people. At the time, I knew I lied because of fear. Even when I was physically hurting and felt like the only reason I was seeing spirit was because I was supposed to be dead.

"It was your way of protecting yourself," my father reasoned.

"Bullshit! I lied because I was a coward! I was afraid of having no friends and not being accepted for who and what I was," I said.

"Yes," he said, "But, you continued to face them after they found out that it was all a lie."

"And, my relationship with my younger sister was forever ruined because of it."

"Do you remember what your mother said?"

"When she talked to me about it?" I asked.

"Yes."

"She made me come clean. I told her that I had lied to everyone because of my conversations with spirit and angels."

"And, do you remember what she said?"

"She told me that she was disappointed in me for lying and that I needed to apologize to my sister, who was worried. I had to tell the truth."

"Yes. That was when you started blocking us out."

"I remember. I had only two friends for the rest of my junior year and quite a bit of my senior year," I said. "I hated high school. I was trying to figure out who I was and realizing I couldn't be truthful about any of it because I was afraid nobody would accept that person. In fact, when I tried to be truthful, I could not bring myself to explain that all of the people I had talked about were spirits that had come to me to talk and that I was taking their messages to their loved ones."

"You helped some of those people crossover to the other side by taking those stories," Timothy said. "You put yourself out there to allow the families to have closure."

"Do you remember Larry?" my father asked.

"Yes. I remember him and his brother John."

"You took the pain of their mother and helped her move past the death of her children by bringing their messages, telling her they were your friends. Your mother knew about what you were doing, but you did not share that with your friends."

"Yeah, I know."

"You could have told them all of that information, but chose not to do so," my father said. "Why?"

"I am not sure. I had these relationships with these boys, knowing that they were dead and that I had to give the information to their parents, but I did not have to share all of that with my friends. They already believed I was lying because they didn't know these individuals. And, I would cry for them. Those spirits were so full of life and I had to see how they died. How do I explain to anyone what I see across the points of my current existence?"

"You were already starting to establish the boundaries," Dad said.

"But, I blocked it all out!" I said, my voice rising in volume. "I stopped talking to them."

"Then, you went away to college. You were still hiding who you were, but you wanted to meet people that did not hold your history against you."

"It was still cowardly."

"No, I do not believe it was," my father said. "You blocked out what you knew to be true, moved to a place you did not know, and started over."

"And, I still blocked my gifts."

"And," my father added, "You started having real health issues because you were not being who you were born to be."

"So, my gifts became my illness?"

"Your failure to allow yourself to be who you are caused some health issues, yes," Timothy confirmed. "But, your choice to not embrace these gifts forced you to become stronger. It prepared you to fully embrace them."

"It only took me 40 years!" I laughed as I said it.

"Everything is how it should be," Timothy told me.

That day, I went into work and was told that I was going to be switched from a salaried employee to an hourly wage due to violations to the Fair Labor Standard Act. Everything fell into place for me in the next 6 months. I was going to be leaving the company I had worked with for almost 8 years. In the back of my mind, I knew that it would be a voluntary ending for me. As with any change, fear was the only thing that would keep me from making a decision.

# Chapter 5

My working routine became redundant. I would start work at 7:00 in the morning and work until 4:00 in the afternoon. I would drive home to change my clothes and go to work my massage business. The chiropractor I worked with, Doctor Leo, referred his patients to me and I referred my clients to him. On occasion, he would include the massage in his plan of care and bill it to the insurance. I'd been working with him for three years and he had gained confidence in my abilities as a therapist.

I had started gaining weight after my friend Cally died. At the time, I referred to it as "packing on the insulation." If I didn't love myself, then, nobody else would love me. Then, I would not have to worry about anyone loving me and leaving me. Of course, I knew that was a crock of crap. The problem was not that people didn't love me. It was that I loved them. To the very root of my soul, I loved the people I cared about. So, I would hurt when I lost those people, regardless of the reason why they were no longer in my life. My emotional eating was easy.

That first year after John died, I ate out a lot. I hated cooking for myself. I didn't know how to cook for just one. Yet, I loved to cook. So, when I did cook, I always had enough to share with Bill, or my work friend, Dianne. I used to make her a pan of lasagna for the holidays. Sometimes, I would make her tiramisu, too. Dianne was also a great cook. She would bring me sour cream chicken. We traded recipes and shared our lunch 2-3 times a week.

At the end of 2010, Dianne learned that she had come out of remission and that her breast cancer had metastasized to her bones. She went through radiation and was forced to go on disability in 2011. She was angry that the company would not allow her to work from home, when they began to allow others to do it. She had more of an administrative role and would have been able to do it. However, it would have added additional stress to her situation. I told her to concentrate on her fight. "You are too damn ornery to not go at this kicking and screaming," I told her.

On the day she had her first radiation treatment, I sent her a text message from work that said, "Are you glowing yet? I will go to the window and watch for the neon light coming from the general direction of your house."

Her response was, "My doctor and I are laughing. You're so stupid."

Dianne told me that I was stupid when I made her laugh. It was a term of affection, which I did not take personally. Yet, every time she said it to my face, I would tell her, "Stupid is a mean word." This would only make her laugh, which I loved! She did it with gusto. I used to call her a "brassy broad," because she really was one.

About the time she went on disability, my desk was moved to another area of the call center and I was back into my subject matter expert role, rather than doing quality monitoring. I was still responsible for doing quality monitoring, but I was also responsible for taking phone calls and supervisor calls, training new hires and learning new product information. One of my organizational skills involved employee relations. Valuing my co-workers was huge, as I knew that they were not valued by their employer. This provoked me to create fundraisers for Dianne and other employees that needed it. I would buy bulk packs of candy bars, chips and snacks and set up a snack box. Any money collected went to Dianne. Because she was loved by many, I went through a lot of candy.

Before I knew it, it was September and I was going to court. The day before court, I knew I would not be coming back into the office. I was right. My labor dispute was settled with the stipulation that I had to resign. I did not come back into the office, other than to pick up my boxed belongings. I had a lot of friends at my employer. They were the family that supported me through my infertility issues, second cancer scare, my head injury, the death of my spouse, and the death of one of our best friends, Cally. I had no idea that leaving my job would cause me to grieve. Yet, I got home from my court appearance, sat on my couch, and cried. I had put a lot of energy into my job. I had put a lot of myself into my job. Even though I hated the company, I loved the people. Plus, no matter what anyone said, if you lived a life of passion, everything in that life was personal. It may only have been a business decision to the company, but it was personal to me.

Within the first week, I had lost fifteen pounds. By my birthday two weeks later, I was down twenty pounds. The stress I carried was part of the reason that I packed on the weight. I believed that every painful memory, physical injury, or emotional hurt that was inflicted by me, someone else, or accidentally, was held in my body in the form of excess weight. Even as I wrote this book, I believed it. My self-medication was food, rather than drugs. Yet, this was only the beginning of my self-discovery into my emotional eating issues.

When my husband had died in 2009, it took me a year and a half to process through the 5 stages of grief. It was not until I left my full-time job that I realized that those stages are true with every type of grieving. For the first 3 days after losing my job, I isolated myself and went through a denial period. I told myself, "You did not really just do that, did you?" The angels in my apartment would just listen to my self-incriminations as I asked myself questions aloud. "Are you an idiot? How could you give up your main source of income? What the hell are you going to do?"

It was Johnny who broke down the wall of self-hate and said, "Oh for the love of God, Toni! Just relax! Everything will be just fine."

"How?" I asked him, panicking. "You were the one who told me I couldn't quit my job and do massage full time!"

"That is because I was afraid that we would be in trouble," he said.

"Well," I said sarcastically, "Hello? Am I not going to be in trouble?"

"Calm down and get to work!" he told me.

"What do you mean?" I asked.

"You are not going to figure out anything sitting on your ass at home. Get your butt into the clinic and decide what you want to happen here," he scolded. "You are the most courageous woman I know. You have never let fear stop you from trying."

Although I knew that was not entirely accurate, I did what he said. I put on some work clothes, my "big girl panties" and went into the clinic, after sitting at home for five days. It was Monday evening, and I needed to bring in more clients if I was going to support myself on my own business. My only motivation was that I could not fail, if I wanted to stay housed, clothed and fed. It was time that I showed up for the company that would support me for the rest of my life- mine. This was the only company where I was not just any number. I was number one!

That first week was challenging. I had been running my business strictly on evening hours for three years. I had to come up with a consistent schedule that allowed for day appointments and coincided with the chiropractic hours. I also had to figure out how I was going to incorporate my medium work. I realized that I had been given my gift for a reason- to help other people. It was time that I started to use my gifts to that end.

At the time I began to brainstorm ideas to reinvent myself, the bargaining stage of grief came forward and dragged me through my fear. I used a lot of "if I did ____, would you (God) do ___?" What was this supposed to look like? How was I going to explain to everyone that I was seeing dead people? How was I going to prove to anyone that my gifts were real? I had no clue where to start.

Ultimately, it was John who convinced me I could do this. Every time I started to panic and worry about what everyone was going to say behind my back, he would sigh and say, "Oh, for the love of God!  Get out of your head! Why do you care what others think?"

"John," I complained, "you know how people are! For God's sake, Bill carries his Bible in his pocket and takes every word of it literally."

"So?" he asked. "It doesn't mean he is right."

"You and I both know that he will argue that he is," I said.

"Toni, my dear, you do not have to prove your gifts to anyone. You're only required to give the message to the appropriate person."

I knew he was right, but the fear that I would lose even more of my support system was terrifying. Though, my father assured me that my mother had known about my gifts since birth, I was pretty sure that nobody else did. Yet, the challenge was incorporating it into my existing business without losing clients. "What do I do?" I asked.

John laid there on my massage table with his hands behind his head supporting his neck and his legs crossed at the ankles. I was the only one in the office and I had nothing on the books. "I think you should talk to

Chris," he said casually. "She already knows how accurate you are. She will help you figure this out."

"Chris has already told me to do angel parties, card readings and drawings," I said.

"I know," he laughed. "I was just wondering if you remembered it."

"Yeah, I do."

"She's right. That is what you should do," he confirmed.

"I will have to think about that," I told him.

"You know," John said, as he sat up on the table, "you have already overthought the subject. Just do it, Toni!" He jumped off the table, gave me a kiss on the cheek, and was gone.

"Where are you going?" I asked, annoyed.

He did not come back, but I heard him say, "Fishing with your dad and my grandpa."

"Always fishing," I said with a sigh.

I could hear his laughter fade away.

My menu of services changed to include "angel services". I offered readings with angel oracle cards, drawings and angel parties. The basic pricing was based on what I saw from other people who offered Tarot readings. My confidence in my abilities to draw faces and people was really not where it needed to be, but I figured I could draw other things that I was shown. Further, I was getting better at discerning the difference between the spiritual beings and their messages. Half of the information that came out of my mouth shocked the crap out of me, as much as it did the people to whom I was giving it. So, the art was getting everything incorporated into my business plan.

Next, I needed to start focusing some effort on marketing my business. I needed to get a website and get online. Although I had purchased a logo, had business cards, and online scheduling, it was time for me to shine some light onto my craft. Illuminating the minds of this small community scared me, as I was sure that finding out about all the dead people walking around this earth was going to shock this energetic dumping ground of a town.

About the time I was figuring out that there was more to web design than I wanted to re-learn, Spirit proved to me that there were no coincidences in life. Also, they reminded me that if I really wanted some help, all I really needed to do was ask and have faith that it was already handled. One day, as I lamented to someone about how lost I was trying to figure out why I had to buy a domain name, get hosting, and figure out design; and the next, Doctor Leo was introducing me to a client who wanted to barter web design for massage. I didn't even know that was what I was asking for, but thank the power of the Universe and God, I was sent Scotty.

The website was built and people could find me. Then, I had to find scheduling software that worked with the website. I used Google calendar for some time, until I was getting double booked in a time slot. I felt like a technological idiot. Though, John told me that I had gone to some technical trade school and studied computer hardware and networking. Then, he reminded me that I worked for a technical support department and had built websites before we met. Obviously, I had not retained any of that information. Yes, that was completely gone due to a blow to the head that had happened two years prior. Or, it was possibly gone way before that incident occurred?

When I was not bargaining, or feeling guilty in my grieving, I got extremely angry about the things that were lying forgotten in my brain. I was even angrier that I could not just let go of these lost talents. If they were truly useful to me, why did I not remember? Obviously, understanding how websites work and knowing how to build them would have been very beneficial and cost effective for me.

Though, anger was significant to the grieving of my memory loss, it served no purpose in the loss of my job. If I was angry, it was with the fact that I had to back into the wall and go through it, rather than using the door. I had to wonder why I was angry at all, as that company was not right.

"Well, Toni," I said to myself, "you can run your own company with more integrity than they did."

"Yes," my father said. He startled me a bit. Spirit was so present for me, that I usually could feel my father and John when they came to me. So, when he spoke, he caught me off guard because I had not even known he was there.

Speaking with my dad had become a regular habit since my accident. There was a fair amount of irony in that fact. My father died in his sleep in 1974. After he died, I would have vivid dreams about sitting at a table with him and talking to him. In the dreams, he would come with other people and they would tell me stories. In the morning, I would tell my mother about the dreams and she would ask me questions about the things I would tell her. On one occasion, I remember telling her something and she had said, "Who told you that?"

"Grandma Cerabina," I told her. I had never met my mom's mother, as she had died two years before I was born.

My mother had a strange look on her face as she asked me more sternly, "Who told you this story?" My mom seemed a bit angry, as she was giving me "the look" and was pinning me with her eyes.

"I told you, Mom," I said, quietly, "Daddy came to me in my dream and he brought Grandma."

"Tell me again, what did she say to you?" she asked me, as if I had not told her already.

"She said, 'Ero un guaritore. Tu sei un guaritore. Vedi lo stesso modo che vedo.'" I explained in Italian. I had no clue how I was able to translate the language to my mother in English, as I did not grow up speaking the Italian language. However, in my dream, she spoke to me in Italian and I understood her perfectly. When I told my mother what she said the first time, I told her in English, "I was a healer. You are a healer. You see the same way I see."

My mother's look was stunned. Then, she just said, "I would not be sharing those stories, Toni Marie. I know you have a hard time keeping secrets, but you must keep this a secret."

"Why?" I did not understand why I had to keep my dreams a secret. I did not understand why my mom seemed to be angry with me. "I'm not lying Mom," I said, close to tears. "This was in my dream."

"I know, Honey," her face softened. "But, people will not understand these dreams."

"You do."

"So," she sighed a little, "You can tell me about them."

As I got older, my dad would appear in the house, outside, at events. I talked to him a lot. Sometimes, he would come and sit, reading the paper, while my younger sister and I played games of make-believe. He walked with us to school. He let me know he was there, even though I could not always see him. I kept that a secret, too.

Yet, it was not until I was about twelve when I started to realize that these dead people walking around were actually people that were connected to me or my parents. Sometimes, they were in my dreams. Sometimes, they would wake me up at night and want me to talk to someone for them. When I slept, I would go into a deep sleep. I dreamed in color. Then, when these new spirits started taking me places in my dreams and showing me people and numbers and places, I realized that there was something more powerful happening.

I prayed a lot in those days. My father would listen and tell me he was there. I was a good kid. I had a foul mouth, but I was not mean, unless someone was mean to me. I was teased a lot in middle school. Boys would call me "Ricky Raccoon" because of the dark circles around my eyes. It hurt being called names, as I got very little rest at night because of the constant onslaught of spirit. Then, during the day, I had to deal with bullies who had to hurt me so they could feel some type of power.

My siblings used to tease me about running into walls when I was younger. They would tell mom that I needed my eyes checked. "Toni just walks into walls." How could I explain to them that I was playing with my friends that could go through walls? That was my secret, too.

I had no problem keeping a secret. What I had a problem with was telling a lie. Keeping a secret was a lie of omission. In high school, I lied in order to keep my secret and it made me physically ill. Then, I lied about my illness. Ten years after my mom asked me to lie about my gift, she asked me to confess my lies, while still omitting the truth about why I lied. When I admitted to my sister that I had lied, I did not tell her about seeing dead people.

I did not explain to her because my friends had already told her I had lied. Worried, she went to my Mom to ask her if I really was going to die from some disease. I knew, in issuing an apology and telling her that I had "made it up," that I would never have her forgiveness and that she and I would never have anything close to what we had as children.

The irony of covering up a lie with another lie was clear in this situation. I lied to my friends about having relationships with people that were not even there to them. These relationships were with the dead boys that would come to me and tell me that I needed to speak with someone and give them messages. So, I talked to Spirit half the night and they showed me their life before their death. They gave me their story and their messages. They led me back to their families. I would contact these families in the daylight, between classes, before, or after school, and deliver these messages. I would get headaches from pure exhaustion and nausea from the energy. Sometimes, I would get light-headed. Each lie covered up another lie, because I could not tell the truth.

When I was faced with confessing all my lies, I had a choice to tell the truth and be who I was, or tell another lie about what was really going on so that they would not think me a freak. The lie won. I was too much the coward to say, "I see dead people." Yet, I was sure that if I did say that, everyone would just believe that was another lie. So, I did the only thing I could do. I lied about why I lied and had my father tell me that he was disappointed in me. My mother was disappointed in me because I told people I was going to die from some illness. When she told me to tell the truth, she specified that I was to tell the truth that I was not going to die.

Entering my senior year of high school, I had one friend that was still talking to me. My sister barely acknowledged me. At school, students talked about me being a liar and spread the word about what I had done. Then, at night, I would have my father scolding me and other spirits asking me for help to deliver messages, until I just started blocking. I ignored my father, who was the most persistent one. I was angry. "What use is having this gift if I cannot use it openly?"

"Toni Marie," my father scolded, "you are not to be sharing your gifts! And, what are you doing, going to these families?"

"What am I doing talking to you?" I asked, defiantly. "You are dead too! Am I supposed to believe that I only have permission to speak with you and who you deem important enough to bring forward?"

"You are taking on too much," he warned. My father was angry, but I did not understand why. I was only using what I was told was a gift.

"Then, maybe," I said angrily, "I should just stop talking to you, if you aren't really there? What about the bad stuff I see? Should I talk to that?"

Somehow, this argument was the reason I shoved my gifts down into the recesses of my brain and locked them away for 22 years. I cannot even tell you how I did it, as I do not remember. However, I know that it was the argument with my father's spirit that slammed the hatch door down with a loud bang. I refused to have any more conversation with Spirit. I was just figuring out who I was and was forced to become something else, and I blamed my father.

## Chapter 6

Sometime before I left my full-time job, I was asked to go to a friend's place in River Falls, Wisconsin and do an angel party. I had already been telling people that I was offering them and had given out some tentative pricing. I had planned on just drawing renderings of the guardian angels and spirit guides, but decided to offer readings with oracle cards. In fact, I had been doing some individual readings already.

As I suspected, there were a few people in my circle who started throwing out the Bible passages about witchcraft. Basically, they were stating that I was practicing "the work of Satan." In these instances, I reserved the eye-rolling for my private conversations with myself. Not that I did not know that Satan existed, as I was seeing demonic energy, just as I saw angelic energy. Yet, I knew people who practiced Wiccan ways and the majority of them were not summoning the devil to do harm. Further, I knew Christians that were not really emulating Christ in their daily life practices, either. I remembered my Catholic-convert father stating, one Sunday after mass, "Everyone is Christian until they get to the parking lot of the church." I was five years old and had a hold of my father's hand, while he carried my sister, Angela, and we crossed the parking lot amidst the "mass exodus."

As this party was my first official Angel Party, I was a bit nervous. "Will I actually get valid information?" I asked my guides before I left my apartment. "Or, is this just a stupid pet trick?"

"Oh for the love of God, Toni," John exaggerated from the passenger seat of the Jeep. "Tell me how many times, since your head injury, have you gone out in public and not seen ghosts or angels?"

I sat, quietly, trying to recall one time since I opened the door to my "gift closet" that I had not seen spirit. John took my quiet as an acknowledgement that he was right, as he continued, "Exactly! Remember? I used to call you crazy?"

"I cannot always understand the messages that I receive for people," I explained.

"Well, you don't have to understand. THEY do," he said.

"You don't have to be so smug about it," I laughed. "So, I just let it come in the head and out the mouth and don't filter it?"

"You are much too kind and careful for that!" he laughed.

"What do you mean?" I asked.

"People will receive messages they do not want to hear. They will receive information that may seem negative to them. However, you know it isn't a bad thing, as we don't see it as good and bad. We see it as the will of God. You've already set the intention that they receive what they need and have put protection in place to clear the bad juju."

"So," I asked, a bit surprised, "that intention stuff really works?"

"Of course it does! You know that! It really is all about intention."

We drove for a little bit, with only the radio noise. Then, I asked him, "Have you actually met Jesus?"

"The Prophet?" he asked.

"No, the Hispanic convenience store clerk that was killed in a mugging," I said, sarcastically. "Yes, Jesus Christ, the Son of God."

"Yes. You have talked to him a couple times, too."

"Yeah, I know," I agreed. "We had a couple conversations on reincarnation, Satan and the witchcraft thing."

"How'd that go?" John laughed knowingly.

"The man speaks in tongues and riddles! How do you think it went?"

His smile hit his eyes, as he joked, "Truthfully."

"Still the smart-ass," I told him. However, I was laughing, too. He was right, it really did go truthfully. Jesus was patient enough to explain it to me, several times, with several examples. Then, he told me that there was "room for science in religion and vice versa."

"Debating with Jesus can make for an interesting afternoon."

"I was not debating!" I protested.

"Yes, you were, Dear. But, we all do it."

Before I could protest again, I pulled up in front of my friend's house and the subject was dropped. By the end of the night, I had only had one of the guests present a problem. John told me that I was having issues because our stories were very similar and that I identified too closely with her messages. However, I did tell the guest this exact thing before I talked to John on the way home. He pointed out that my intuition came through for me in that moment and I trusted that the reading I was giving was for her, not me.

"It is interesting," I said, as I drove carefully into the night, "how I trust everything I get for others, but question everything I get for me."

"Yes," John said, "you have to get out of your own way and stop rationalizing the answers you receive. It really is about faith."

"I guess it is. Then, I think that I am being a hypocrite if I tell someone to step forward with this blind faith and trust that God and their angels have their back, but won't do it myself," I pondered. "Is that just fear getting in the way?"

"That is mainly why you have doubt. However, sometimes," John went on, "it is just your ego."

"My ego?" I asked.

"If people knew that they had the answers all the time and just had to trust their gut, there would be a lot more happiness in the world. People just worry about everything and focus on the negative stuff. Can you possibly throw caution to the wind and just follow your intuition?"

"John," I laughed, "I don't think I ever heard you string so many sentences together when you were alive."

"Now, who's the smart-ass, Toni?"

"I think that probably was your ego," I laughed. Growing more serious, I asked him, "Were you afraid too? Were you afraid of what everyone would think of you?"

For a moment, there was a silence in the car that felt weighted. He did not say anything. Then, he said, "I was always picked on. But, it was rare that I fought back. I didn't have to believe what people said to me, or about me. I knew the truth."

I wished at that moment that I could learn that lesson. Then, I realized that was the ego. That part that needed to fight and prove everyone wrong. The truth was,

John was a good person and he never cared what anyone thought about him. He just went about his business. Whereas, I cared way too much what others thought. I always had a need to defend myself and those around me. I needed to get involved. And, when people tore me apart for nothing more than their need to do it, I had a hard time letting that go and not internalizing it.

The silence that had fallen in the car was broken when John said, "Toni, the reason why you are questioning everything, now, is because you are fine-tuning your gifts. They have lain dormant for close to 20 years and you have been hiding who you really are. Now, you are stepping out of your hiding place. There will be a day, when you will not fear being who you were meant to be. Just be patient and know that you can trust your gut, just like you trusted the information you were giving to the people at the party tonight."

"Well, I am trying to do just that. Be who I am and trust that I will come out on the other side of all this unscathed."

"Oh, you will pick up more wounds to your heart. Some of them will be inflicted by family, and other scars will come from people who you will love more than you thought you could love again. Just take the lesson and try to tell your overthinking brain to let it go."

I knew what he was telling me. I knew this information was foreshadowing heartache and pain through love. On one hand, I knew how awful it would be for me to lose my heart again. On the other, I felt hopeful that I could possibly love someone as much as I did him.

The smile spread on his face, as he was in my "overthinking brain" seeing my thoughts. "Oh, yes," he said, "there will be another man who you will love as much as me and give all your heart to him. It's my job to make sure he is worthy of it."

"But, you said I will be hurt again? I don't think I can handle shooting another spouse out of a potato launcher." I was trying to ease my worry, remembering what I had done with some of John's ashes two years prior.

"Dear, you cannot help yourself. You love, almost automatically, and there are many men out there that will not be worthy of that enormous gift. However," he continued, "The one that is will be strong enough to walk by your side, or be in your shadow. In addition, there will be one who is strong enough, but will walk away a coward, blaming it on everything but what it is."

"Shit!" My complaint was loud.

"Remember," he said gently, "You cannot recognize the right one until you see the wrong one. You cannot have one without the other. You know that."

"Can't we just skip the losers and get to the winner?"

"Well, there is still a chance that one of the losers will be a winner because of the whole free will thing. Besides, the losers will be the ones that will regret their decision. You will be the best thing to happen to them in their lifetime and if they let you go, they are the idiots."

It hit me then. He had said "losers" rather than "loser." There was going to be more than one of them. I was going to have to go through the whole heartache of dating, loving and breaking up again. I hated that part!

A part of me hoped that I would remember this conversation when I was meeting the losers, but I knew I wouldn't. John was right. I loved easily and cared too much about people. I knew that I could love anyone who showed me love and accepted me with my gifts. It would be the ones that chose to leave me that would cause the worst scarring. I did not want that again. It took me 33 years to find John. If I had my heart broken again, I knew that I would never love the same, if at all. I would need to be done.

"You won't be done. But, you will get very hurt."

"Quit doing that!" I said to him, annoyed.

"What?" he asked innocently.

"Reading my thoughts! You're responsible for sending me the next husband anyway," I practically yelled. "So, you better make him a good one, dammit! And, if he's not, I am going to find you when I get there and kick your ass!"

He was laughing about that when I pulled into New Richmond. "Stop at Kwik Trip and get some ice cream, or you are going to have to come back for it," he told me.

"What?" I asked.

"You know you want some ice cream. Just stop on your way home. It's only 11:30 and tomorrow is Saturday."

I laughed, as he still knew me pretty well. The temperature outside could be below zero and I would still eat ice cream. It was my treat of choice, next to chocolate. So, I drove into the lot of the local Kwik Trip and went inside. One of the workers there was a younger man with sandy blonde hair and glasses. I had seen him on other nights that I stopped and had talked to him a couple of times. That night, I was a bit burned out and just smiled, told him to have a good night after paying for my ice cream and left. John waited until I was letting myself into the apartment before he said, "Yeah, you think he's cute and too young for you."

"Yes, I do," I responded, knowing he was speaking of the associate at Kwik Trip. "There is something about him that just feels…I don't know."

"Familiar?" John suggested.

"Yes!! Exactly!"

"Did you feel that way about me?" he asked.

I thought a moment and realized that I had felt that way about him. "I felt like I had known you before; almost like déjà vu. Definitely the same feeling I get with him."

"Just remember," John advised in a light tone, "free-will changes everything. We all have the power to be angels or demons. Even Satan made the choice."

It was Uriel who spoke then, as he said, "Some people would argue that the Bible says Satan was cast out of Heaven."

"Was he?" I asked. "Or, did he make the choice to leave?"

"What do you think?" the archangel asked me.

"I do not think a merciful Father would throw out a son whom he created because he was misbehaving, especially if that Father was the creator of all things and created those things in his likeness. That would be a complete lack of self-love, if he was really casting out spirits."

Maybe I was overly tired from channeling spirit that night, or just imagined the reaction? I was not sure which was true. However, when I looked up from dishing some ice cream into a dish for myself, I saw that John, Archangels Uriel and Michael, and Saint Germaine did a head tilt in unison to the same side, like dogs do right before they start begging for your food. They were just staring at me. "What?" I asked, as if my response was completely normal.

"You have a lot of confidence in your answer," Uriel said.

"Well," I began, pausing long enough to take a bite of Chocolate Dream ice cream, "I am. I do not know why I feel that way. But, I would be lying if I said that I felt like God would smite me for what I am doing now, even though the Bible says I am some evil person because I talk to you guys." I swept my spoon out in their general direction as I sat down in my recliner chair. "Free will is the same as intention to me. I am not summoning evil on anyone. I don't claim to be a fortune-teller, do I?"

"No, you don't," Michael acknowledged with a grin.

"The only reason why I am offering these parties is because you guided me to do so. I asked God for help and he sent you. I am not supposed to waste my gifts!" I said with conviction.

There was a collective nod and Michael said, "No, you are not. And, you know that these gifts are from your Divinity, but you question them."

"True," I said, "but, I also question how my gifts will not allow me to pick the winning lottery numbers. Plus, which of you told me that 'what we resist, persists'?"

"You read that in a book," Michael said.

"Maybe I did, but is it an inaccurate statement? I tried to block out my stuff and suddenly, I get my bell rung and I have all you guys talking to me again. Or, should I push this stuff down and deny my gifts?"

"First, you will not ignore your gifts anymore. You cannot do so and still fulfill your purpose," Michael explained. "Second, just because you are embracing these gifts, it does not mean that every teaching you had from the Bible studies in catechism was not valid. The stories there are meant to guide you to make a decision with your heart and soul."

As he talked, I listened and thought about how to respond. "Yet, are they real?" I asked. "Are they really the words of God? Or, how about the Koran? The Torah? Are they any more or less the word of God?" Apparently, the sugar was kicking in and giving me the energy to question these Angels.

Uriel held up a hand to quiet me, "You know the answer. You have known it for many lifetimes. You've had countless conversations with Jesus, us, and God, or what some call 'Source Energy'. What do you say the answer is, Toni?"

In the two and a half years since my head injury, I had many conversations with all of the spirit entities that Uriel named and more. Uriel was one of the toughest ones to argue with, as he was pretty set in his ways. However, he was passionate and truthful. Somewhere in my studies, I read that his name in Hebrew was translated as "fire of God," or "the one who is most like God." When he asked point blank questions, it was hard not to cower a little. I had to act as casual as possible because showing weakness in my response would be less than honorable to my gifts. "I believe that these documents are interpretations of what God said through his messengers. I believe they are stories that happened to others, and that it is up to each individual to decide how to incorporate these words into their relationship with their spirit and the spirits of others. All pathways lead to God, or Source. And, I also believe that we have the choice to practice these beliefs for the highest good of others, or to use these words to condemn the actions of others for our own righteousness."

Again, the doggy head tilt from the four stooges amused me enough to continue. "I don't believe there is a wrong or right answer here. I believe it still comes down to a choice and free will."

"Do you believe in Heaven and Hell?" Uriel asked.

"Yes," I admitted. "However, I also think we experience both because of choice. I don't think we are condemned to one or the other."

"Why do you think that?" he asked, almost smiling.

"Because, there have been many things that I have gone through in this lifetime that forced me to choose to keep going or quit. Those are dark times, when you cannot see any light in a situation and just want it to be done. You just want the emotional, physical, and mental pain to stop. Some people lose all hope and in that instant, they are in Hell. And, Satan is right there waiting for them, trying to convince them to stay in Hell, or expand it by pulling others into it with them."

Uriel, Michael and St. Germaine nodded their heads, acknowledging that some of what I had said was valid. Yet, they never actually said anything to indicate it was correct, it felt right to me. For some reason, I felt that was all that mattered.

# Chapter 7

By the end of October, I had a plan and my website had been up and running for a few months. I was learning how to use my online scheduling and was managing a more regular schedule, though I still worked a lot of late hours and was not getting my morning schedule filled. I believed that had something to do with New Richmond being a commuter town. Most individuals that lived there did not work there, unless they owned a farm or a business in town.

In addition, I had another angel party that was booked at the party I had in July. This party was in Spooner, Wisconsin, which was 75 miles north of where I lived. This time, I was more excited than nervous. I was gaining confidence in my abilities to talk to the guides that were with other people. Evidently, they were eager to speak to me too. When I went out in public, I often had them approach me, asking if I would talk to their loved one for them. Yet, I had set my boundaries when I started to reclaim my gifts and everyone was shut down quickly. "You get them to come to me, or you go away," I would tell these spirits. "If they are open to receiving these messages, you will have to help them find me. When they are ready, they will come."

Aside from the parties, I had been doing readings for people on a one-on-one basis for over a year. On a couple rare occasions, I was asked to give readings when out with my friends and family members. I had discovered that it was harder for me to stay grounded when I was drinking, so if I started to give readings to people at parties, I had to quit drinking. Further, if the individual that I was giving a reading to was intoxicated, or heading in that direction, the angels, guides and spirit that were with them took on a different role and were not always willing to give messages. From what I was told, the main job for the angels and guides became protecting the individual from taking on energy that was not theirs. Apparently, the addiction to alcohol and other substances left a door to our spirit open and unprotected. At the time, I thought it a plus that I no longer smoked or drank regularly. Sure, I still had an occasional glass of wine, a beer, or a Long Island, but I gave up the smoking habit I had taken up after John died when I left my job. Plus, smoking marijuana and other substances left holes in the energy field that most people never repaired. As these habits become more important to an individual, the theft of the individual's spirit becomes harder to avoid for the angel.

"Why is that?" I asked one day of nobody in particular.

It was Archangel Uriel who responded to my question. "How do you fill your well?" he asked me, as a response to my question.

"My spiritual well?" I asked to clarify.

"Yes."

"I try to do things that allow me to connect," I explained, "art, walking, meditation, prayer and other stuff."

Uriel nodded his head and began, "remember when John died and you started smoking cigarettes, thinking it was the lesser of two evils?" When I nodded my head, he continued, "At that time, you were choosing to smoke so you did not have to think about being alone."

"What?"

"Think about it, Toni. You went outside for smoke breaks because it was social. You said it yourself that you were an OP smoker."

He was right. I was an OP smoker, which meant that I smoked 'other people's' cigarettes. I did not buy my own because I refused to smoke in my car, or my home. Occasionally, when I did buy my own, I ended up sharing half the pack, or the pack lasted me a week. I smoked to keep my hands busy because if my hands were busy, I did not think. When I paint, I only think of the painting. When I walk, my mind wanders, but I do not obsess about any topic. In those moments of disconnection, some of my most amazing connections to spirit happened. Yet, when I smoked, I let go in a different way and my connection to spirit was harder.

"So, to clarify," I said, "I cannot connect with spirit when I am drinking or smoking because my energy goes to that substance?"

"Well, yes and no. The concept is right, but it is not always about substance. That substance of choice could be a game, the television, your phone, or that thing you call electronic mail," Uriel said. "It is anything that distracts you from what you are meant to do."

"Anything that distracts someone from purpose?" I asked.

"That and anything that distracts you *with* purpose," Uriel clarified. "That is free will. You chose to smoke, which is free will. However, you also chose to quit because you are more connected to your spirit and Divine energy than before your accident and you are clear that you are supposed to do this. You are no longer repressing your gifts."

"So, are other people repressing their gifts by doing these things?" I asked.

"Yes. Though, they may not know it and that may be part of their purpose."

"Why do these conversations bring more questions than they answer?" I asked, not really expecting an answer.

"If you did not question, you would not learn," Uriel responded.

"That was a rhetorical question!" I said, exasperated.

He actually laughed at me. "No, it wasn't."

I redirected back to the topic at hand. "So, having an addiction to a substance is part of their purpose?"

"It could be. Your choice to not drink after the death of your spouse was learned from one of your past lives, when you were a drunkard."

The word 'drunkard' made me laugh. "I was a drunkard?"

"Oh yes! Many times."

"So, why would I decide not to be a drunkard in this lifetime?"

"I realize that word is not used in your present time," Uriel sighed. "You are only repeatedly saying it now because you are being a smarty pants."

"You mean a smart ass."

"Yes."

"Can you not say it?  Can you not use swear words?"

"Why do I need to?" Uriel asked.  He was grinning when he said, "You use enough of them for all of us."

"If you had a British accent, I would say that answer was 'quite cheeky'."

"You are a clever one.  But, just remember," Uriel said, "I'm older than you and far more clever."

"Is that like dog years?" I asked.

His eyes actually twinkled with a fire or gold and blue, which was very cool to watch.  "If you are the dog in this scenario, I would still be older, Pup.  I shall call you that going forward."

I could hear a chorus of laughter from the other angels, though they were not presenting themselves.  "Oh great," I said in a voice dripping with sarcasm, "another nickname!"

"Well, it is better than some of the nicknames you had when you were younger."

"True," I conceded.

This conversation with Uriel was always in my mind when I was having a drink, or with others who were drinking. When I went to the party in Spooner, Uriel refreshed my memory about the alcohol.

The angel party was so much fun and very busy. The hostess had all types of snacks and beverages. Individuals came in and out of the house to socialize. Some of the individuals received readings while others did not. It amazed me how spirit showed up for people in many different ways. In addition, some of the people that showed up had messages that were similar, but different. That was when I first recognized that angels could appear differently for each person. For example, Archangel Michael appears for me as a large, dark-haired man with a square jaw and a huge sword. When he came in with someone else, I knew it was him by how he felt, even though he presented with blonde hair and softer features.

The other thing I learned was that guides and angels did not always give me a name to associate them. Sometimes, they allowed me to call them whatever I wanted. Other times, they would tell me, "My name is not for you to know." This led me to advise the individuals who were receiving the reading to ask for a name before they slept. The angels and guides would supply their name to the individual's direction in the morning. Often times, it was the first name they thought of when they woke up. However, I have clients that have experienced different ways in which they received the names of their guides. I, too, have received the names in unexpected ways. One time, I was getting a massage from my friend Cally, when two guides came together. One of the guides was a very large, grey wolf that called himself Tzar. He had golden eyes, the color of a tiger's eye gemstone. He was quite impressive. When he spoke to me, his voice came through in a rich, deep baritone in my head. Tzar was with a red-headed angel named Paula. She was beautiful in a sparkling, bluish- silver dress and was introduced by Tzar.

Regardless, I believed that I received exactly what was meant for the individuals at the party and left around ten thirty that night. I had been reading for close to twelve hours. My drive home was dark and slow, as I was watching for deer the whole way. I had been drinking water most of the day and had to make a couple stops at gas stations. By the time I got home, it was almost midnight. I was tired and hungry. I went in the house, looked in the fridge and realized there was nothing I wanted to fix to eat. After quickly checking the freezer and finding it without ice cream and frozen pizza, I grabbed my keys and headed to Kwik Trip, which was a block away.

I walked in and noticed that the young cutie that I liked to flirt with was working. I grabbed a carton of mint chip ice cream and some frosted brownies. I was going to buy a frozen pizza too, but realized that it was almost one in the morning and I was going to go to bed after my brownie sundae and a shower. I was not about to stuff myself on a frozen pizza, too. I grabbed a couple bags of milk also. For some reason, after I got over the concept of milk in a bag, I found that I liked it better. The milk stayed colder and did not get a funny taste from the container it was in. Not to mention, milk-in-a-bag was less expensive. I could buy a gallon of milk-in-a-bag for almost a dollar less than a gallon of milk in the plastic jug.

"Any fuel out there?" the cutie, who wore a name tag with the name of Chris, asked me.

"Not tonight. I fueled up in Cumberland," I said.

"Cumberland?" he looked at me questioningly.

"I was doing a party up in Spooner today," I explained.

"Like a multi-level marketing type thing?" he asked with a grin.

My energy level was in bad need of the brownie sundae, so rather than get too far into it, I said, "Yeah, something like that."

"Ah, gotcha," he said. He nodded and grinned, showing me his dimples. Then, he winked at me.

A little dumb-struck by the flirtatious, sexiness of that unconscious wink, I just stared for a couple seconds. I was asking myself if I thought he realized he was doing it. I don't even remember what my mind came up with, but knew I had to move. "Thanks Chris," I said, using his name.

"See you next time," he said, winking again as I stepped away from the counter with the bag he had handed to me.

"Do you always work this late?" I asked, as I usually saw him in the evenings.

"Yes."

"Well, see you next time," knowing that my next evening run to Kwik Trip would probably be the following Tuesday. As I got into my car, I realized that there was more than a pull of attraction to him. I had some form of soul connection to this gas station cutie that I was not aware of until he winked. The flirting was just that, as I knew he was married and was just giving as good as he got. Yet, in the short drive around the corner, I realized that I was flirting too. It was like training for a marathon that I had no intention of signing up to run. I was not even sure that I was ready to date anyone.

"Why the hell not?" John asked, as if I had said this aloud.

I was putting my key into the deadbolt lock on my apartment door when he just appeared next to me and startled me. "Would you stop doing that!?" I said in an angry whisper. The lights in my neighbor's windows were dark, so I knew they were sleeping. I did not want to wake anyone up by yelling at a ghost that nobody else could see.

John chuckled, as he knew he had startled me. In fact, that was probably his intent all along. I put the milk in the fridge and the ice cream and brownies on the counter. I took off my jacket, draping it over the kitchen chair. "I didn't realize that spirits could be jackasses too," I said to him. He chuckled harder.

I took a brownie out of the plastic container and put it in a bowl, which I put in the microwave for 25 seconds. When the timer went off, I put two scoops of mint chip ice cream on top of the melted frosting and put the carton in the freezer. The melted frosting was like hot fudge in the sundae and the brownie was warm enough to soak in the melting ice cream. I sat down on the reclining chair and turned on the television. Within seconds, my fat, black cat, Nova, was on my lap looking for an ice cream hand out. "Nova, you cannot have this," I said. He head butted the hand with the spoon. "No."

"He is so spoiled!" John said.

"Well," I said, my mouth half full of ice cream, "we never had children."

John nodded, saying, "I am sorry about that. I said things to you that were not very fair."

I just shook my head, knowing that I was too tired to begin this conversation. "God had his plan for us. For me, babies were not part of the plan."

"One day, you will be grateful."

"I'm grateful now, John! I would be raising a child alone. It's bad enough that Brooke still has growing up to do and you are not here. I cannot even imagine having a child of a younger age to raise without you."

"You would have been fine," John assured me. "You turned out fine."

"My mother is a saint!" I said, with a laugh. "If we had adopted or had one of our own, I would be no good to that child now. I am feeling too lost, still."

"Pup," Uriel said, "finish your treat and get in the shower. You need rest."

I sighed at the use of my new nickname. "Yes, Sir," I saluted him with my spoon.

"John, you know your purpose and are needed elsewhere," Uriel said in a reprimanding voice. It sounded like John was goofing off and got caught.

"Okay," John said, and kissed me on my cheek before he left.

"Thank you," I whispered, knowing that Uriel was effectively ending the conversation for me. "I know he could still be here and there at the same time."

"True," Uriel nodded. "But you are in the need of sleep. The emotion that conversation would have invoked was far more than you needed to deal with tonight. Get to bed, Toni."

With that, I finished my ice cream, quickly showered and went to bed.

One of the things that I did before I left my employer and lost my health insurance was have a sleep study done. I was having issues with not feeling rested when I awoke in the morning and thought I should get checked. The whole time we were married, John was somewhat of an insomniac. On a couple occasions, he told me that I stopped breathing in the night and that I snored like a lumberjack. After he died, Nova would wake me in the middle of the night by standing on my chest and blowing in my face. My cat was twenty pounds, so just standing on my chest should have been enough to get me moving.

In addition, I had really bad edema in my legs and felt that I was going to die when I worked out. Aside from being incredibly out of shape, I had started making poorer diet choices out of convenience and a lack of ambition to cook for one. John loved to eat, so leftovers were rare, prior to his passing. It was easier for me to eat prepackaged crap than make a meal that normally feeds four to six people and eat it for five days. I was okay with eating one meal of leftovers. However, eating four meals of leftovers made me want to binge on crap and eat ice cream and brownies for dinner before bed.

When I had my sleep study, they put a CPAP on me within forty-five minutes of going to sleep. After getting used to breathing with a mask on, I had the best night of sleep I had had in a long time. When I received the results of the study, I realized that Johnny's insomnia was probably due to my sleep apnea. According to the information obtained from all the electronic stuff attached to me, I stopped breathing 112 times in one hour of sleep and the lowest my oxygen level got was 52 percent. I was suffocating my heart and setting myself up for a heart attack, high blood pressure and many other health-related issues because of my sleep deprivation.

So, I sleep with a Continuous Positive Air Pressure device that keeps me breathing throughout the night. When I sleep, I am rested. My blood pressure improved and so did the edema in my legs. As long as I was wearing my mask, I didn't snore and I slept very well. Whether I obtained four hours of sleep or 8, I felt better rested and less emotional. Further, I started to remember my dreams and some of the conversations I had in my sleep with spirit.

When I woke up on the day that followed the angel party in Spooner, I was going to my Mom's for family potluck. I had gone to bed around two in the morning and woke up around 9. I remember thinking that I would have been in worse condition if I had not discovered the benefit of wearing a CPAP to bed and getting quality sleep. Who cared if I looked like an alien with the mask and tube strapped to my head? My cat slept between my legs and left me alone all night, only waking me when he wanted breakfast.

After showering and dressing for my afternoon at my Mom's, I put a salad together to take with me as part of my contribution to family dinner. As October was the month we celebrated my birthday, I was not required to bring anything. However, I remember that I had volunteered to bring a salad. I did not have dressing, but figured my Mom would have something at her place. I knew we would have stroganoff, as that was my favorite and I had requested it. In addition, we were having white cake with ice cream and hot fudge rather than birthday cake. Again, I requested it. The salad was a nice addition.

My mom decided that having a potluck once a month was the only way to get all of us together regularly. Everyone had their own life. Mom was often alone and she never wanted her children to lose each other after she was gone. She wanted her children to still have family, which so many other people lose when their parents die. As with any family, we were frequently on opposite sides of issues and did not always get along. Mom never wanted a rift between us that would become a chasm of distance that we were too stubborn to cross. In addition, she understood her children well and knew that we could be each other's worst enemy and still have each other's back in a fight.

Before John died, Mom had called a family meeting for just her biological children. "It is not that I do not love my sons and daughters that married my children, or my grandchildren, but what I have to discuss involves my children." My mother had seen too many families torn apart from petty arguing over things that had been assigned value. "When I die, I do not want anyone arguing over my dishes! I do not want you kids not talking to each other because of possessions. We all hear the same thing together, write it down, and it is done. Nobody argues because we hash it out now."

At the time, my relationship with some of my siblings was tentative at best. In many ways, I felt that I could not live down past wrongs and that I would never have any relationship with them that was sustainable. I was different. I always had been and felt like I was on the outside looking into the window at a party where I was not invited. In many ways, I felt that way in John's family, too. I wasn't invited or accepted. But, I loved him and he loved me and that was really all that mattered. My mom loved me unconditionally. When I did something wrong, she let me know she was upset and it was in the past. Yet, a couple of my siblings could hold a grudge for years. For that reason, I understand why my mother felt it necessary for the six of us to hear the same thing at the same time and be on the same page. She did not want any of us to disown the other because someone got the formal china set my mother used for Christmas dinners.

In October of 2011, at the family potluck dinner, I realized it was time to start getting rid of some of John's stuff. Nothing that belonged to him would ever bring him back. Those were just possessions. The memories and the love that I had for John did not come from keeping his things. I held those things in my heart. It took family dinner to realize this.

When John came into my life, we started doing holidays together. The worst holiday to coordinate was Christmas. My family tradition was always celebrating the December birthdays on Christmas Eve and Christmas on the morning of the holiday. My sister, Brenda, celebrated her actual birthday on December 24$^{th}$. However, there were seven December birthdays in our family and they were all celebrated on the 24$^{th}$ with Brenda. This conflicted with John's Mom's Christmas get-together with her children. John's Dad typically celebrated the weekend before with his children. In the ten years we were together, I missed my family potluck on Christmas Eve. The year before John's death, his mother, Ann, started going to Texas in October and staying through the holidays. Then, the Geving Christmas moved to Christmas Eve and I did not feel it was right that John would have to miss that day.

It was while I drove to my Mom's that October when I realized I was going to separate myself from the Geving holiday tradition. Brooke was old enough to coordinate her involvement with her aunts, uncles, grandmas and grandpa. Though I still regarded them as my family and loved them all, I did not believe I still had a place with them. It was not that they made me feel unwelcome. They still invited me to participate. My reason for not going was that someday, I knew I would have someone new in my life and it would not be fair to him to expect he split his holidays with me, my family, and the family by marriage to my late husband. I asked John about it as I drove and he said, "My Dad and Shari will get it. They will understand. But, you know how my mom and sisters are. I don't think they will understand."

"John, I cannot continue to split my time," I said.

"As I have said before, why do you care what anyone else thinks? You can still do social things with them and not have to do the holidays."

"So, this will probably be the last year I do the Christmas with the Gevings," I resolved.

"It will probably be next year that is your last year," John stated.

"We will see," I told him.  I thought about this. When I pulled into my mom's driveway in Bloomington, Minnesota, I realized that I was letting go and trying to move on with some hope that I would not always be going to dinner alone.

# Chapter 8

The end of December was warmer than it usually was in Wisconsin. We had a little blast of snow before the holidays and a blast of cold the weekend after Christmas before the New Year. In my family tradition, we welcomed Christmas morning.  My step-daughter, Brooke, had moved back into the apartment with me in the end of September.  In the two years since her father had died, she and I went through multiple challenges because of our grieving.  The bottom line was that we both needed each other.  Despite all the issues between child and step-parent, we loved each other and wanted the other to find happiness. We both operated from our hearts, which caused us pain over and over again. Not everyone leads with the intention of love, but Brooke and I did.

One of my brothers lived in Ohio and came home for the holidays, usually after Christmas. So, we had mom and the children under eighteen years of age open their gifts when he and his family came. In 2011, we celebrated Christmas on December 30$^{th}$. The only reason I remembered this was because I shared a ginger brandy with my sister-in-law, Bonne, to toast John's birthday. It was a Friday night.

After I got home that evening, there was a knock on the door. I signed for an envelope and the messenger left. The envelope contained a notice that the apartment had been sold at auction and that our lease would terminate by January 15$^{th}$. The options stipulated in this notice were to vacate by January 15$^{th}$ and receive money to relocate, sign a new lease at a new monthly rate, or buy the building. I called the realtor Monday, asking about what the rent would be and the asking price of the building. Although I did not want to be a landlord, it was an option that I needed to explore to make an informed decision.

Unfortunately, the realtor could not tell me anything about a lease because he had not sold the building.

Further, he would not give me a cost to buy the building. He left me with no other option but to move, and nobody was renting apartments in January. After much debating, I asked my mother-in-law, who was wintering in Texas, if Brooke, Nova, and I could stay in her trailer home until she came home in April. I agreed to pay the utilities and pay for the cable. I was very grateful to her for accommodating me.

While John was alive, there were times when his family and mine seemed less than supportive, the way families can be. There were many times when one of my in-laws accused me of "thinking I was better than all of them," which could not be further from the truth of what I felt. I would not have said that I agreed with all of their behavior or responses to every situation, but I never thought I was better than anyone. John and I had many discussions about the things that were said to him and I about the other. John would blow it off and say, "That is a reflection of them, not you. They feel uncomfortable because you call them out on their own bullshit."

However, I have received a lot of help from family in the years after his death and have been grateful. I was given a loan of money from his sister and brother-in-law to help me when I had an incident of identity theft. They allowed me to repay them in massage. I repaid a loan to his mother in the same way, in addition to paying her back money she had loaned me. It may have taken time, but I did repay the loans with equal service. All of the other stuff that happened and hurt my feelings was part of the grieving process on both sides. Although I have written about incidents, I have never bashed anyone for their involvement nor said they do not have the right to grieve in their own way.

If I have learned nothing else, I have learned that our reactions, accusations, and explosive moments have more to do with our own issues. Families bicker and fight. They point fingers, pass judgment, place blame and say things that hurt. At the end of the day, they are still family. Sooner or later, we all have to lay down our weapons and choose to walk away from the fight- if for no other reason but to heal our own hearts.

With the help of my family and friends, I moved my household of 10 years. My furniture and 90% of my apartment went into a storage unit. Finally, I cleaned out the crap in the garage and got rid of the junk. Everything I touched invoked a memory of John and I needed to be selective about which ones I kept. I loved my husband, but he was a pack rat! I gave away dishes to my sister-in-law, Julie, who wanted them for her cabin. I sent Brooke to Goodwill with household items, her car loaded to the roof.

My friend and her son came over and helped me pack my dishes into cartons, wrapping them in paper. I was grateful for the assistance I had from all of my family and friends.

In addition, I was grateful for 50-degree temperatures in January that year! We were blessed beyond belief that we were not packing up stuff to move through snow and ice. On January 15, 2012, I handed over the keys to the apartment I had lived in for ten years and walked away with hope that the changes coming would not break me. We were settled in the trailer and were going to try to find some new happiness. An hour after I handed my keys to the creepy realtor, it started to rain and the temperature began to drop. Yes, we had been blessed.

At some point within a month of my moving, my storage locker sprung a very large leak. I had gone into the unit to get something on a rainy day and there was water pouring from the ceiling onto my sectional couch and sofa sleeper. Neither of them was salvageable, and my renter's insurance was not covering it either. About the same time, my computer died. I felt like 2012 had come in with a middle finger saluting me. I had resigned from my full-time job, lost my home, my furniture and my computer. But I was still standing and commuting 30 miles to work, and somehow, I knew I would make it.

In the middle of February, my mother-in-law informed me that she decided to come home earlier than planned. Although she said that Brooke and I could stay there with her, I was not comfortable doing that and started looking for another place near New Richmond, where my massage practice was located. I wanted to be moved out before the end of March, when Ann would be returning. With the help of friends and family, we moved back into the city in the middle of March. I signed a six-month lease at a price that was more than what I was comfortable paying on my own. As Brooke was living with me, she agreed to pay half the rent and stay for the six months.

With the help of my father-in-law, Jack, and my brothers, I moved my washer and dryer, and other furniture out of my dysfunctional storage unit on Saturday, March 17th. It was Saint Patrick's Day and it was eighty degrees outside- a totally, freakish event for Wisconsin. Unfortunately, this holiday was a huge deal in this small town. There were quite a few Irish that lived there, which demanded all kinds of tomfoolery. Every year, the town had a parade and green beer at the bars. When John was alive, he even proclaimed himself Irish and jokingly called himself Paddy O'Furniture. By the time everyone left, I was ready to just sit still and relax for some time. I offered to buy dinner for everyone, but they were ready to leave by 5 and had already spent more time helping me than they had planned because of the parade and having to go to a hardware store on the opposite end of town for some part for my dryer.

The two-bedroom townhome I moved into had a two-car garage and a small walk-out patio. It was within walking distance of the chiropractic clinic and the apartment I lived in with John. I liked it, even though it was more expensive than I could afford.

I remember that the utilities were crazy. In New Richmond, the electricity was part of a cooperative energy buying system. I paid over $150 a month for electricity, water and sewer for a two-bedroom apartment. The cost of living was rising and most wages were declining. For many people, the year of two thousand twelve was brutal financially. I was still making it work, though it was challenging. I was grateful that Brooke was working and paying her half of rent.

Although we did see each other in passing, Brooke worked odd hours and was making friends with people from work. I was happy that she was socializing with new people that seemed to understand the need to be responsible. How quickly we learn the value of our hard-earned money when we have to pay for those things our parents used to buy for us. Although, I wanted her to go to school, I realized that was completely up to her. My mom used to tell me that the only way she could help me go to school was to give me room and board while I paid for my own education. That was what John and I had conveyed to Brooke before he passed away. John and I both appreciated our education more because we had to work hard to pay for it.

One of the other reasons why I was not pushing the college thing with Brooke was that I knew she was not ready. Although John and I went to college, neither of us finished until we were in our forties. There were individuals in my life who thought that was a bad thing and asked Brooke, in front of me and John, "Do you want to be like your father and still be in school when you are forty?" Looking back now, I think I would tell them that it is never too late to expand on an education. In addition, I would point out that I worked harder because it mattered to me. John graduated from college with a 3.95 GPA, was working one full- time job, a part- time job and making time for the people that mattered. Personally, I was proud of him for going for it and doing so well. Who cares when your birthday is?

Although, I knew Brooke was a bright, young woman capable of excellent work, I also knew she was still figuring herself out. In many ways, her self-esteem kept her from realizing her full potential. She believed what people said about her, rather than showing them that they were wrong in their assessment. Plus, as with most of the young adult population entering colleges, she was not looking for a career she loved. Rather, she was looking for a career that would make her a salary that showed her success. If you have to work for your education, you are more likely to take it seriously if you are passionate about the field. Simply put, Brooke had not found her passion.

Without a doubt, I was passionate about what I did. I figured this out shortly after I overheard my nephew telling his uncle, "Why doesn't she just get a real job?" I do not remember why he was saying that about me, but I knew that had to have come out of one, or both, of his parent's mouths. It amazed me that people thought that about my profession! Quite frankly, it really pissed me off when I heard him say it because I knew he was repeating what he had heard.

At the time, I was working for myself, marketing my business, building my client list, paying for supplies, and creating websites, logos, advertising and branding my work without a support system at home. I had gone to school, graduating with over 910 credits in massage in less than two years, obtained National Certification and state licensing while working a full-time job and my part-time business. Regardless of anyone's opinion, my work was worth so much more than they would ever know or understand! I did not do it for the money, for recognition, or fame. I did it because I was meant to do it and I loved every minute of it! How many people could say that about their jobs?

When I posted a comment on social media that night, my sister-in-law called me to tell me that she did not think I had any business putting that on my page. "I think Facebook should be for positive messages." I did not even name my nephew in my post, so it confirmed for me where my nephew would get such a notion that what I did was not a "real job". The best decision I ever made was giving up the benefits, the boss, and the desk in the cube farm! Granted, the work was hard and sometimes, did not make rent, but it was far more valuable because I care about my clients and my number one employee- me. No job has ever given me that peace of mind! Plus, no company would give that to anyone on their payroll!

I did the right thing. I was trusting my gut on this one. It was hard, but it was worth it.

www.ingramcontent.com/pod-product-compliance
Lightning Source LLC
Chambersburg PA
CBHW051656040426
42446CB00009B/1164